ONE WORLD:

THE LORD'S PRAYER FROM
A PROCESS PERSPECTIVE

BRUCE EPPERLY

Energion Publications
Gonzalez, Florida
2019

ISBN10: 1-63199-642-8
ISBN13: 978-1-63199-642-9

Energion Publications
P. O. Box 841
Gonzalez, FL 32560

energion.com
pubs@energion.com

TABLE OF CONTENTS

A WORD OF CAUTION AND
CONSOLATION

The words "be careful what you pray for" could surely apply to the Lord's Prayer. Truly embodying this thirty second mantra could transform your life. It could "afflict the comfortable," by challenging your assumptions about God's presence in the world and your calling as a follower of Jesus. This prayer is not for the faint hearted. Grounded in the prophetic traditions of Israel, the Lord's Prayer forces us to reflect on our image of God, personal and political ethics, finances and professional goals, and relationships. The Lord's Prayer compels us to reflect on our deepest values and requires us to live in accordance with our ultimate allegiance, as Bob Cornwall counsels.

The Lord's Prayer can also "comfort the afflicted" by reminding us that in maelstrom of history and conflicts of everyday life, God is with us, providing us with bread for the journey and resources for personal transformation. Those who pray with Jesus awaken to a holy adventure, a world of unanticipated possibilities and new freedoms with God as our companion and guide.

A Chinese blessing — or is it a curse? — pronounces "may you live in interesting times." Nothing could be more descriptive of the current planetary, political, and personal environment. We are overwhelmed by "breaking news" and are, whether we like it or not, global citizens, shaping and being shaped by events emerging in real time from Washington DC, Moscow, Beijing, or Southern California. There is nowhere to hide, even if we go "off the grid." The planet is peril, with signs of global climate change abounding, and the nation is in peril as polarization has replaced shared values and politicians fan the flames of mistrust, racism, and violence, often with the complicity of religious leaders. We need a wider perspective from which to view the breaking news of each day and discover creative and healing resources to address our personal anxieties and our communal alienation.

I have chosen process theology as a lens through which to understand our Savior's Prayer. Although you will find only a smattering of theological jargon in this text, my own personal spirituality and understanding of Jesus' Prayer is grounded in the vision of a relational, open-spirited, profoundly personal, always creative, and forward-looking God, who invites us to be companions in the holy adventure of healing the earth. Process theology embeds us in the world of embodiment, nature, relationships, and politics, and within the circles of our lives, process theology invites us to be agents of creative transformation, guided by God's moment by moment vision of possibility. From a process perspective, "there is no other." We are joined in an intricate fabric of relatedness in which our calling is to be the change we and God want to see in the world. We stand on holy ground, with our Heavenly Parent giving us guidance for bringing healing and wholeness to this good earth. God's will is for us to be agents of beauty, justice, and love, using our freedom and creativity to bring heavenly values to earthly challenges. Though both the Lord's Prayer and process theology are profoundly God-centered, their message is clear: because our times are in the hands of a lively, intimate, healing, and just God, we are the ones we have been waiting for, as poet June Johnson reminds us. If heaven is our destination, we must first make the earth heavenly, embodying generosity, forgiveness, holiness, wisdom, and praise in our daily lives and political involvements.

This text emerged from a seven-week sermon series, preached during the summer of 2018, when USA leaders separated children — even babies — from their parents as a deterrent to immigration, demagogues threatened catastrophic war, fires raged and temperatures soared as signs of global climate change, and political leaders incited hostility, fear of strangers, and racial and cultural division. Now more than ever we need Jesus' wisdom and guidance. We need the Lord's Prayer as our personal and corporate GPS "for just such a time as this."

I am grateful to my Cape Cod congregation, South Congregational Church, United Church of Christ, for its intellectual curiosity and care for the neighborhood and the planet. I am ever thankful for our congregation's affirmation of my vocation as a theologian-writer-pastor. I am thankful for the growing number of prophetic voices rising in our time, reminding us that heavenly values need to be brought to earth in feeding the hungry, comforting children, seeking justice for the marginalized, and saving God's beloved planet. I also want to thank Bob Cornwall, John Dominic Crossan, John Shelby Spong, and N.T. Wright, whose short books on the Lord's Prayer companioned my own reflections. May God's will be done, God's vision be birthed, on earth as it is in heaven.

CHAPTER ONE
TEACH US TO PRAY

Jesus was praying in a certain place, and after he had finished, one of his disciples said to him, "Lord, teach us to pray, as John taught his disciples." He said to them, "When you pray, say..." (Luke 11:11)

"Pray then in this way." (Matthew 6:9)

Prayer is at the heart of human experience. Prayer is what Ann and Barry Ulanov describe as primary speech. Persons in every culture and faith tradition, dating back to the beginnings of the human adventure, have called upon a power or wisdom greater than themselves in times of crisis and need. It's been said that there are no atheists in foxholes, and I believe that even atheists pray. The skeptic and atheist cry out in the night for relief and healing; express hope as a loved one faces surgery; and shout for change in the face of injustice. Prayer is universal, requiring no particular ritual, words, belief system, or community.

As we begin our reflection on the Lord's Prayer or our Savior's Prayer, we need to explore the meaning of prayer. As a young child, I grew up seeing the phrase "prayer changes things" whenever I opened the refrigerator door. I suspect my mother wanted to remind her two boys about the importance of prayer. I also believe that she was addressing her own need to live prayerfully as she faced the daily demons of depression, low self-esteem, and obsessional thinking. My mother believed that even in her darkest hour, when life seemed intolerable and there was no way forward, God would get her through, and make a way when she could find no way ahead.

I believe that prayer is the ultimate form of connection. When we pray, we discover we're not alone in the universe. We may not know to whom we're praying, but we hope against hope that Someone is listening and that this Someone, whose presence and activity has brought us to this point, will respond to our current expressions of gratitude and need. Dag Hammarskjold, the famous General

1

Secretary of the United Nations, describes a prayer connection that transformed his life:

> I don't know Who – or what – put the question. I don't know when it was put. I don't even remember answering. But at some moment I did answer *Yes* to Someone – or something – and from that hour I was certain that existence is meaningful and, that, therefore, my life, in self-surrender, had a goal. From that moment, I have known what it means "not to look back" and "to take no thought for the morrow."[1]

Prayer awakens us to the graceful interdependence of life. When we pray, even if we don't have the right words or can't articulate the force to whom we pray, we confess that we didn't get here on our own. Our current life situation, gifts and talents, and achievements are grounded in a Graceful Interdependence without which we could never do anything or be anything. I believe that this Graceful Interdependence refers to the loving power we describe as God, "the One to whom all hearts are open and all desires known." This is the Holy Energy of Love, undergirding, guiding, empowering all creation, and constantly inviting us to claim our own freedom and creativity as God's companions in healing the world.

Lessons in Prayerfulness. The Lord's Prayer is a lesson in prayerful connection. It is obviously not the only way to pray, but it provides a path to prayer in the interdependent, and dynamic world in which we live. In Luke's Gospel, Jesus teaches the prayer in response to the disciples' quest for a spiritual practice that uniquely reflects Jesus' mission. They do not question the validity of John the Baptist's prayer. They want to learn a prayer form that speaks to their condition and context, that embodies Jesus' message of God's One Kingdom or Realm. In Matthew, Jesus is more didactic in providing spiritual guidance, "pray then in this way." In either case, there are times in which we believe we need a spiritual road map, a spiritual GPS, to connect with the Wisdom, Power, and Love of the Universe. The Apostle Paul confesses our need for spiritual guidance in Romans 8:26-27:

---

1   Ibid., 205.

Likewise the Spirit helps us in our weakness; for we do not know how to pray as we ought, but that very Spirit intercedes with sighs too deep for words. And God, who searches the heart, knows what is the mind of the Spirit, because the Spirit intercedes for the saints according to the will of God.

Recognized or not, the apostle proclaims, the Spirit is praying within us, but not just us, the whole creation "groans" in anticipation of healing and transformation. (Romans 8:22) We live, as Psalm 148 affirms, in a world of praise in which all creation lifts up its voice to our Creator. Inspired by God who prays within us, our prayers are never private, but reflect the prayerful interdependence of all creation.

Author Anne Lamott provides an initial lesson in prayer. Lamott sees the movements of prayer as "wow!", "thanks!", and "help!" To Lamott's instructions, I would add: "sorry," "inspire," "awaken," and "connect."

"Wow" – A sense of wonder is at the heart of prayer, wonder at the reality of life itself in all its complexity, grandeur, and tragic beauty. Rabbi Abraham Joshua Heschel says "radical amazement" is at the heart of spirituality. If you aren't amazed or filled with wonder from time to time, you really aren't religious. The heavens declare the glory of God and so do our immune systems! Think a moment – what are your "wow" moments?

"Wow" is connected to "thanks." In a recent adult faith formation class at South Congregational Church, we sang "I thank you God for the wonder of my being...I thank you God for the wonder of all being." We are truly, as Psalm 139 avers, awesomely and wonderfully made. Each moment is a miracle and each breath an inspiration. Dag Hammarskjold prays:

For all that has been – thanks!

For all that shall be – yes!

Thanksgiving joins us with the Graceful Interdependence of life. We are all part of an intricate and dynamic fabric of relatedness in which there are no self-made persons. We are agents who make choices and achieve goals, but all these actions depend on the grace of our planetary environment, pivotal people, and helpful circumstances. I am here today because of loving parents who valued education, supportive mentors, and my birth in a land of opportunity. If you aren't thankful, you can't be faithful. As the German mystic Meister Eckhardt counsels, "if the only prayer you can make is 'thank you,' that will suffice." In gratitude, we find our spiritual path and inspiration to seek justice and healing in our world.

"Help." Ann Lamott is a recovering alcoholic. She knows she needs help; she knows that she is powerless in relationship to her addiction without the grace of God that inspires our own agency and strength. We all need help. In the Graceful Interdependence of life, God is constantly reaching out to us in "sighs too deep for words" and synchronous encounters. In asking, seeking, and knocking, we discover that all the resources we need are in and around us and in our relatedness to God and the whole earth.

"Sorry." Nothing could be further from the truth than cliched words from the film "Love Story" – "Love is never having to say you're sorry." We all have secrets, we all have missed the mark, we all have forgotten important things, and either intentionally or unintentionally hurt others. We have all sinned and fallen short of God's vision for our lives. The Psalmist prays:

Search me, O God, and know my heart;
test me and know my thoughts.
See if there is any wicked way in me,
and lead me in the way everlasting. (Psalm 139:23-24)

Confession opens us to divine energy and personal power. Confession is an act of interdependence reminding us that what we do matters, that we are agents whose lives affect others, and that we can "repent," change direction and become larger, more compassionate persons. Confession reminds us that what we do individually and corporately as churches and nations also matters to God, shapes God's experience, and causes God suffering as well as joy.

"Inspire." We need a vision of the future. We need a far horizon to guide our steps. Content even with a positive present, we slip into mediocrity. When we quit expecting greatness from ourselves – and greatness can simply be doing ordinary things with a loving spirit – we begin to decline and rust from the inside out. We need to capture God's vision for this moment and our world.

"Awaken." Following the death of Michael Brown in Ferguson, Missouri, the Black Lives Matter movement surfaced the phrase "Stay Woke." Followers of Jesus are called to be "woke" people – sensitive to injustices committed in our communities, whether on the borderlands, city streets, and school playgrounds. When we pray, we ask where we need to be awakened to "what's goin' on," as Marvin Gaye sings, in our current social situation.

And, finally, "connect," — prayer connects. We often deny or are unaware of the profound interdependence of life. Politicians speak of "nation first" and moguls proclaim the gospel of "self-made men" — yes, men! — and "rugged individualism." Yet, in the spirituality of Jesus, no one is more pitiable than the self-made person, who emulates the man who built a great barn and congratulated himself on his achievement, only to die that very night! We are joined in an intricate fabric of relationships. Agency and achievement go hand in hand with receptivity and interdependence. In the body of Christ, described in 1 Corinthians 12, "If one member suffers, all suffer together with it; if one member is honored, all rejoice together with it." This is Paul's dream for the church, where we are all joined, but it is also the community and the world. As prayerful people, we pray, "Connect me with your power and love, and join me with the world around us."

Prayer is primary speech, and even if we don't know how to pray, God's spirit is already praying in us in sighs too deep for words and guiding and awakening us, even when while we're asleep.

Prayer challenges us to grow, as Jesus did, in wisdom and stature. One of my professors, Bernard Loomer, who coined the phrase "process-relational theology," saw stature or size, our ability to have spirits large enough to embrace difference and diversity while keeping our spiritual center, as the central religious virtue. Prayer connects us with the world's joy and sorrow and enlarges our spirits, inspiring us to move from self-interest to world loyalty. In this spirit, I close with a prayer cited in *Deep is the Hunger* by one of my mentors, African American pastor, theologian, and spiritual guide, Howard Thurman.

Each night my bonny, sturdy lad
Persists in adding to his,
Now I lay meDown to sleep,
the earnest wistful plea:
"God, make me big."
And I, his mother, with greater need,
Do echo in a humbled, contrite heart,
"God, make me big."

Yes, God make us big in thanks, wonder, connectedness, and compassion. Make us big in prayer.

LIVING THE PRAYER OF JESUS

Recently, a number of variations on the Lord's Prayer have been written, reflective of the unique gifts of culture and faith in our time. I believe that these variations add to our understanding of Jesus' prayer. Accordingly, I invite you to live with the following prayer in the spirit of the Lectio Divina or Holy Reading. My version of the practice involves the following steps:

Find a comfortable place and take a few moments for silence, breathing deeply and gently.

Pray for God to guide and inspire your reading and reflection.

Read the passage, scriptural or non-scriptural twice, letting the words soak in.

Listen for divine insight or inspiration, without censorship. Guidance may come in the form of a particular word, song, image, relationship, or person.

Meditate a few minutes on this insight.

Ask God to guide you to greater understanding of the message God has given you. Give thanks for God's inspiration every moment of the day.

Take time to live with this version of the Lord's Prayer from New Zealand:

Eternal Spirit
Earth-Maker, Pain-bearer, Life-giver,
source of all that is and that shall be,

Father and Mother of us all.
Loving God, in whom is heaven.
The hallowing of your name echoes through the universe!
The way of your justice be followed by the peoples
of the earth!
Your heavenly will be done by all created beings!
Your commonwealth of peace and freedom
sustain our hope and come on earth.
With the bread we need for today, feed us.
In the hurts we absorb from one another, forgive us.
In times of temptation and test, spare us.
From the grip of all that is evil, free us.
For you reign in the glory of the power that is love,
now and forever.
Amen.

Throughout the days ahead, pause to reflect on this prayer along with a traditional translation of the Lord's Prayer from Matthew or Luke.

CHAPTER TWO
THE PARENT OF US ALL

"Our Father who art in heaven,
hallowed be your name."

I was blessed to have a loving father, who read with me every morning, played ball with me after school, and encouraged my education and professional life. I have tried to embody his positive parenting in the integration of my personal and professional life. For me parenting and grandparenting is a vocation, involving protection, nurture, character-building, and love, for my own family, the children of our church, and children throughout the nation and planet I'll likely never meet. At a certain time of your life, you move from self-interest to selflessness, and are willing to give your time, talent, and treasure —— even your life — for the well-being of a child or grandchild who is truly bone of our bone and flesh of our flesh. In many ways, the relationship of parent and child is our primary example of selfless and sacrificial love.

At the heart of the Lord's Prayer is Jesus' invocation of God as Abba, a term used to describe the intimacy between father and child. The God Jesus prayed to is not distant and demanding, preoccupied with rules and regulations, and ready to pounce on our slightest mistake. The God Jesus prayed to is like the best of parents – loving, patient, listening, and guiding, willing even to die for the well-being of the child.

In calling God "Abba," Jesus raised the bar for our images of God and our images of parenting. A good parent aspires to be godlike in her or his loving and protective care for vulnerable and impressionable children because this is the way the God of the Universe behaves. The Infinite is the intimate, and loves us more than we love ourselves.

The Loving Parent. North African theologian Augustine asserted that God loves each of us as if there is only one of us. Divine universality is joined loving intimacy. God's love is like a circle whose center is everywhere and whose circumference is nowhere, fully present to each of us, God loves all of us. In a universe of 200 sextillion stars like our sun, God is fully present in every life. Every child is loved, each child is cherished, all children are documented by their Heavenly Father. God is present in all things and all things are present in God.

Some have suggested that a better translation of "our Father" is "Father or Parent of us all." In a world in which we build walls that separate friend from foe and insider from outsider, God sprints to welcome every child. All are loved by the "Parent of us all" who inspires us to love one another, especially those from whom we are alienated.

"Who art in heaven." Now I don't believe that Jesus' invocation of heaven is intended to be a geographical description, but rather a way of describing God's unique universality and ultimacy. "Heaven" describes God's moral nature, vision for the world, and transcendence over every finite perspective, even that of Jesus' followers. God is not at our beck and call, though like a good parent God hears our prayers and responds lovingly. The intimate God is also the ultimate God, beyond anything we can control or fully imagine. God's ways transcend our limited perspectives, loyalties, and prejudices. In focusing on heaven, we orient our spiritual GPS toward God's values and priorities, and God's vision of wholeness for ourselves and others. Heaven points us, as Bob Cornwall affirms, to our ultimate allegiance, transcending our idolatries of God and country, race and religion, and doctrine and ritual.

Knowing the Parent. Historically, our concepts of God have vacillated between two poles – God as known and described by us and God as mysterious and beyond any words we can say. The God in heaven cannot be encompassed by human speech and symbol, or church and ritual. God is not a male, God is beyond gender, and so may also be appropriately described as "Amma," our loving mother. As Brian Wren's hymn affirms, we can "bring many names" to describe the good shepherd, rock of ages, light of the world, spirit of gentleness, majestic creator, and suffering savior. No one word can contain the God of this and every other planet, galaxy, and universe, whose creativity spans 13.7 billion years, and on to infinity in every direction. We can stammer with the author of Psalm 8 as we view the immensity of the universe and the grandeur of God, "What are we humans that you are mindful of us? Who are we that we matter to you?" And, with this same wordsmith, we can proclaim that the God beyond all things is also within all things, creating us to be "a little less than the angels." The Infinite is the intimate, the universal is the incarnational.

Heaven is the great beyond that reminds us that God transcends our self-interest, moral categories, and national aspirations. Abraham Lincoln captured our sense of God's ultimacy when he said, "Let us not pray that God be on our side, but that we be on God's side." In describing Aslan, the Lion King of the Chronicles of Narnia, C.S. Lewis noted that "Aslan is not safe, but he is good." Lewis' fable *The Lion, the Witch, and the Wardrobe*, Aslan describes God's goodness and power by Aslan's dying to save a wayward boy and then rising to vanquish the powers of darkness.

Nations rise and fall. Kings and Oligarchs, thin-skinned demagogues, come and go, strutting on the stage of life, but God's word endures forever, and God's vision calls us to challenge the morality of every nation and asks us to claim our role as God's image by going beyond self-interest to world loyalty. The one whose eye is on the sparrow has the whole world in his hands and loves us fiercely with mother's love. "Heaven" is our destination, not as geography, but as our aspiration to bring heaven to earth and put God's way ahead of our small-minded ethics and politics. We take God's name in vain when we reduce God to our politics and self-interest or assume that God favors our nation, church, political hero, or beliefs at the expense of others.

The Infinite and Unnamed is also the ever-present companion. Absolute in love, God is also relative in companionship. Unchanging in intentionality, God is ever-changing in personality. New every morning, God is constant in fidelity. God loves this world as a parent loves a child and we love God by loving the world God created and still creates with each new day. Loving God, we love the world rightly, and go beyond our need to dominate, control, or diminish; loving the world, we take our role, following our Loving Parent, as God's companions in healing the earth.

A Relational God. While this one passage could take all summer to unpack, let me add one more way of looking at our divine parent, the father and mother of us all. Good parenting counsels and guides, and protects, but it also listens and empathizes. Alfred North Whitehead once asserted that God is the fellow sufferer who understands. Two millennia before Whitehead, Jesus said that as you've done unto the least of these, you have done unto me. What we do matters to God. God is empathetic, the great heart of the universe is touched by all things. A good parent's heart breaks at the sight of a profoundly ill child or a child dealing with issues of mental or emotional health or addiction or a child intentionally separated from her parents. God feels our pain more than even the best of human parents; God embraces our pain and rejoices in our joy. God is the heart of the universe. And, God needs us to be partners in bringing beauty to this world. The calling of our Heavenly Parent is "Do something beautiful for me. Give me a beautiful world, not an ugly one," for our loving parent needs children of compassion and purpose, who – within every task – reflect our parent's love and share our parent's vision of healing the world.

Abba, Amma, the beloved Parent of us all, the parent of our Savior, with whom we pray, "Our Heavenly Parent, let me be like you, loving and large-spirited, willing to sacrifice to heal the world.

LIVING THE PRAYER OF JESUS

Read meditatively the words from Psalm 8, describing the grandeur of God and the apparent insignificance of humankind. Take some time for silent reflection on this passage. What images of God are most inspiring to you? How do you understand the Holy One? Where have you experienced God in your life? Visualize the Holy One's presence in your life and the world. In the stillness, invite God to refine your images of Divinity and expand your sense of God's presence in your life. Take some time to ask, seek, and knock in expectation that God will respond to your deepest aspirations and guide your steps so that you might do something beautiful for your Creator. What questions or requests do you feel

11

called to make to the Holy One? Ask God to bless your questions and aspirations so that you might align yourself with the Heart of the Universe.

CHAPTER THREE
HEAVENLY MINDED
AND EARTHLY GOOD

"Thy kingdom come, thy will be done,
on earth as it is in heaven"

Rabbi Hillel the Elder, the great spiritual teacher of Judaism who lived in the century before Jesus, counseled:
If I am not for myself, who will be?
If I am only for myself, what am I?
If not now, when?

No doubt Jesus was aware of the Hillel's wisdom as he charted his ministry. Yes, God cares for each one of us and wants us to flourish. The One who notes the fall of the sparrow and numbers the hairs of our head knows our deepest needs and wants to respond in ways that bring wholeness to our lives. Our prayers for our needs matter to God and help us discern the difference between need and want, and world loyalty and self-interest. God cares for all of us and wants every child to experience life in all its abundance. Children of the Divine Parent seek the healing of creation in its intricate and dynamic interdependence. Spiritual maturity takes us beyond individualism to sacrificial living for the greater good of our neighbors.

When Jesus says, "thy kingdom come," he is invoking the prophetic vision of Shalom, the peaceable realm in which everyone has a home, the streets are filled with the laughter of children, and every nation follows the path of justice.[2] Jesus' mission statement

---

2   Many today prefer to use "realm" or "community" as being less patriarchal and more inclusive. I agree with this intent, although I have used the more traditional language in this text as a way of reflecting the prayer language of most Christians. When the kingdom of God is seen as all-inclusive, it goes beyond patriarchy to community.

from Luke's gospel provides a context for the world he imagined. Following the prophet Isaiah, Jesus proclaimed:

> *The Spirit of the Lord is upon me,*
> *because he has anointed me*
> *to bring good news to the poor.*
> *He has sent me to proclaim release to the captives*
> *and recovery of sight to the blind,*
> *to let the oppressed go free, to proclaim the year of the*
> *Lord's favor.* (Luke 4:18-19)

You notice how earthly Jesus' vision statement is: it embraces the totality of life, both individual and corporate. Rooted in the prophetic tradition, it includes legal, economic, and governmental policies. It's about poverty, amnesty for those imprisoned by Rome, healing of physical ailments, liberation from political and relational bondage, and freedom from slavery. Jesus' use of the year of "God's favor" sounds vague to our ears but it meant something to Jesus, Isaiah, and their communities. It was the Jubilee Year, God's awaited year, the forty-ninth and fiftieth year of the cycle of seven sabbatical years. In the Jubilee year, the economic order was turned upside down, debts were cancelled and properties returned to their original owners, breaking the cycle of poverty and closing the gap between the rich and the poor. There is no ultimate distinction between the spiritual and physical and sacred and secular; all things are interdependent in God's realm of Shalom. There is only one kingdom — God's realm of Shalom — and we are challenged by Jesus to do everything we can to bring this realm to our daily personal and political relationships.

Contrary to many popular theologies today, there's nothing about going to heaven in Jesus' mission statement. It's about the holy here and now and bringing justice and healing to this good earth. You don't have to go to heaven to be in heaven. An omnipresent and omni-active God is always creating a heavenly world right where we are. With Jacob, we may wake up, and notice heaven on earth, and then exclaim in retrospect, "God was in this place and I did not know it." If we take care of this world, we can trust the next world to God.

As Martin Luther King asserted in his "Letter from the Birmingham Jail," there is no separation of body and spirit, earth and heaven, and spirituality and economics in the biblical tradition. Perhaps, King remembered not only Jesus' vision statement and the prophets of Israel, but that his mentor – and one of my mentors- Howard Thurman, stated that the mystic's encounter with God as a living reality inspires her or him to confront anything that prevents people from encountering God.[3] The mystic challenges laws and social practices that stunt spirits, destroy dreams, separate families, and plant seeds of despair. The mystic realizes that spiritual wholeness requires just societies as well as inspirational religious teachings.

The Will of God. "Thy will be done" is at the heart of Jesus' prayer. Many people interpret God's will in terms of an all-determining power or fate. They see the will of God as God's choice in matters of life and death, salvation and damnation, health and illness, and victory and defeat. We hear invocation in "if it's God's will, I will survive the operation" or "God chose my candidate as president," or "it was God's will that the plane went down with no survivors while I had a flat tire and missed my flight." I don't believe that this is what Jesus meant. Although God is present in every moment of our lives as the source of inspiration, possibility, and energy to live our dreams, "God's will" — here in the Lord's prayer — is about "God's vision," "God's hope," and not some inscrutable working out of divine destiny or fate.

New Testament theologian John Dominic Crossan claims that when we pray "thy kingdom come, thy will be done, on earth as it is in heaven," we are saying we want to bring the values of heaven to our daily lives and our nation's priorities. This is an aspirational prayer in which we ask to be "heavenly minded and earthly good," embodying by our lives God's heavenly dream. Heaven is the fulfillment of all things, the fully healed world, that God wants right now and not in some far off, ethereal sphere.

---

3 In using "him" and "her" and "he" and "she," I recognize that these terms do not fully embrace the non-binary realities of many of God's children. Our language needs to catch us with our ethics and spirituality, but we still have a way to go, and I am wrestling with the most inclusive language for our emerging diversity.

Over a hundred years ago congregationalist pastor Charles Sheldon wrote the social gospel classic *In His Steps*, which charts the lives of a group of persons who covenant to ask "What would Jesus do?" whenever they are confronted with a decision. Asking that simple question changed their lives — they now looked at their daily decisions from a heavenly perspective. Business was not just business; it was about "good work" and care for laborers. Relationships were not just about fun but service and affirmation. Government was not just about staying in power but about seeking justice and serving the least of these. In other words, bringing heaven to earth. In Sheldon's time, following God's will involved preventing alcohol addiction, confronting poverty, and supporting worker's rights. Today, it is also about protecting the environment, enacting policies that protect children, ensuring the well-being of vulnerable persons, responding to homelessness and addiction, and making decisions that unite rather than divide. It is appropriate when we pray, "thy will be done" to ask "What is God's will for me to do in this situation? What is God's will for our church in our decision-making? What is God's will for national and public policy?" The answers aren't always easy and we may have to compromise, but God always guides us.

LIVING THE PRAYER OF JESUS

This chapter's exercises are two-fold in nature. First, I invite you to participate in an imaginative prayer. After a time of prayerful silence, begin to visualize yourself entering the "gates of heaven." What do you experience? What do you see? What is the nature of relationships in heaven? Experience yourself as part of a heavenly community. Then, in the spirit of Hillel, ask yourself how might you be part of making this community come to pass "now." Ask for God's blessings on your meditations and for the inspiration to live out your heavenly vision in daily life.

The second exercise aimed at making the heavenly vision come to earth involves, in the spirit of Charles Sheldon, asking the question, "What is God's will for me to do in this situation? What is God's vision in this situation? How can I live out God's vision in the moment and the long haul?" Process theology affirms that God has a vision — or many visions — for each moment of experience, reflecting who we are, our life experiences, and the context in which we find ourselves. Spiritual growth involves attentiveness to God's vision — the array of divine possibilities — for each moment and embodying them in our unique and personal way, using our own freedom and creativity.

CHAPTER FOUR
BREAD FOR TODAY

"Give us this day our daily bread."

I love good bread. San Francisco sour dough bread, Italian garlic bread, corn bread, and raisin bread. My heart is filled with joy as I bite into a scone or croissant or dollop a large smear of cream cheese with lox and capers on an "everything" bagel. Where there is bread there is life and where there is bread, there is celebration.

Jesus counseled, when we pray, let us remember to ask God "give us this day our daily bread." Bread is the stuff of life and the symbol not just of celebration, but survival as families face starvation, malnutrition, and drought, much of it the result of political chaos and climate change. Bread is incarnational. It is the body of Christ, and in its breaking, we know that Risen One is our companion.

Scholars debate the exact meaning of "give us this day our daily bread." Some scholars believe that Jesus is referring to our daily need for sustenance and security. Others prefer the translation, "give us today the bread we need for tomorrow," suggesting that Jesus was referring to our need to place the future and its uncertainty in God's care, rather than succumbing to anxiety about what is out of our control. I believe both answers are right.

"Give us the bread we need for today." The meaning of this prayer is elusive to middle class and upper middle-class North Americans, who pick up a week's worth of groceries as we pilgrim from Trader Joes to Whole Foods and the supermarket, with a mini-stop at a liquor store on our way home. We have full cupboards and freezers, and bread in our bread baskets. But, in Jesus' day, and in some parts of the world today, adults went to the market every day. Then and now, millions live one day at a time, making just enough money to buy today's or tomorrow's groceries.

I confess that I am a person of privilege, who sometimes needs to declutter my refrigerator and cupboards of stale or "beyond the use by" foods. But, I have been poor, and being poor shapes the way I look at life, even though I have more than enough today. When I was eleven, my dad lost his job and we had to leave my childhood garden of Eden, our small town, and move to the big city. I recall our family getting food baskets and living from paycheck to paycheck till my Dad got back on his feet, first as a security guard at $3 an hour and later after he recovered his professional career, and my mom went back to school to renew her teaching credential. Many years after our brush with poverty, my mom confessed that my father considered suicide during this time, believing he was "worth more dead than alive."

I can empathize with persons experiencing homelessness and unemployment, the single parent scraping by, the out of work trades person, and the inner-city teen locked in a cycle of poverty. It astounds me when I hear people uttering "the poor are lazy" or "if they only had a work ethic, they would succeed." Or use the passage "the poor are with you always" to do nothing to respond to poverty here and abroad while rewarding the wealthy with tax cuts. I am sure that God doesn't care how you got into trouble, God wants to get you out.

Jesus knew the meaning of daily bread. He fasted for forty days in the wilderness, and no doubt longed for a crust of bread, as he sought to discern his vocation.

We pray for bread enough for today, and we pray for tomorrow's bread as well. Many of us fear the future and ask "will we outlive our retirement plans, and what will happen if we get sick?" These are real fears, and I share them as I find myself in my mid-sixties and not as agile as I was 40 years ago and have discovered that "better living through chemistry" no longer applies to going on the Beatles' Magical Mystery tour. Yet, in our fear and anxiety about the future, Jesus reminds us to consider the lilies of the field and birds of the air. If God takes care of these, won't God supply our deepest needs as well? The problem is that for many of us our wants have become our needs and our luxuries are viewed as necessities.

Daily bread is a big deal, and my love for bread and the good life has led to having to concern myself with diet and weight. I have the health anxieties of the affluent, those who eat too much and own too much. But, there is another weight problem – it is the weight of poverty and malnutrition, the reality that close to three million children will die this year of diseases related to an inadequate diet while millions more will suffer from chronic illness of mind and body due to not having proper nutrition. When Attorney General Jeff Sessions boasted in 2018 that many of the children separated from their immigrant parents on the borderlands had better living conditions than American children, he expressed a terrible truth that should convict every USA citizen – kids in our neighborhoods don't get the right nutrition and kids in rural and urban America go hungry. Just two miles from villas in Hyannisport and Osterville and my own home in Centerville, on Cape Cod, 70% of the children at a local elementary receive subsidized lunches.

When I was a boy, I played the role in a Sunday School play of the boy with five loaves and two fish, whose generosity enabled Jesus to feed 5000 persons. Now, I am sure that Jesus can do great things. Using the dynamic energy of life, the power of the big bang, Jesus can find ways to multiply loaves. When God's imagination is embodied in the world, miracles occur. But, I believe that day another miracle occurred. In this era of growing gaps between wealthy and poor, the vanishing middle class, we can imagine that when the folk in the crowd saw the boy come up with his loaves, they had an epiphany – "if we share – if we let go of our worries about security – everyone, including us, will have enough." And, so they shared and a multitude was fed. The same is true for us. Hunger experts say there is enough food to go around. It's a matter of our willingness to share from our abundance in terms of foodstuffs, educational guidance, and the creation of infrastructures for distribution

Perhaps, you recall a parable describing contrasting images of heaven and hell. A man had a dream: he went into two banquet halls both of which had tables heaped with nutritious and tasty food. In both rooms, large and unwieldly spoons were attached to each arm, such that those eating could not bend their elbows to scoop up the food in front of them. In the first, there were shouts and anger as each person tried unsuccessfully to scoop up the food from his or her own plate. In the other room, there was singing and laughter, each one used their long spoon to feed their neighbor!

Ironically, for all of our wealth, many of us live in hells of anxiety, greed, and isolation. Our nation faces spiritual bankruptcy because we have favored the wealthy and powerful over the "least of these."

There is only one world. The bread of life is physical as well as spiritual. What happens in the halls of Congress and voting booth reflects our relationship to God as clearly as our evening prayers and church attendance. Despite our Christian privilege in the USA, those who fail to hear the cries of the hungry and poor will, as the prophet Amos warns, eventually experience a "famine" of God's word. Rich in things, but poor in spirit, focusing on bathrooms rather than bread, we will *"wander from sea to sea and from north to east; we shall run to and fro, seeking the word of the LORD, but we shall not find it."* (AMOS 8:12, AP)

In our anxiety and hope, let us pray: "Give us this day our daily bread. Give us enough to share with others, for in our generosity, we are fed, and in our sacrifices, we are welcomed to a banquet of divine delight, where our needs are met and everyone is fed."

LIVING THE PRAYER OF JESUS

On her autobiography, *Take This Bread,* Sara Miles tell how she, as an atheist, found herself spiritually transformed when she shared in the eucharist, the Lord's Supper, at an Episcopalian church in San Francisco. Her heart was opened, and like the Emmaus pilgrims, she experienced Christ in the breaking and eating of bread. Transformed by the bread of life, Miles wanted to feed others and discovered her calling in creating food distribution centers for persons experiencing hunger and poverty.

The Psalmist proclaims, *"taste and see that the Lord is good."* (Psalm 34:8) God is present and comes to us through all our senses. As part of your spiritual practice, pray with your eyes and mouth open. Meditatively savor tasty food, eating slowly, enjoying the flavor of a good meal, or a freshly baked slice of bread slathered in your favorite topping. Give thanks for your five senses – especially taste, smell, and sight - and for good food. If you haven't already done so, shift your focus at some later time to the photos of persons experiencing hunger or malnutrition in your community and the world. Let these photos be "icons" or windows to divinity. Let God come to you through these photographs.

Prayerfully discern how you can respond to poverty in your neighborhood and the world. Then, make a commitment to one initial act of care for persons experiencing poverty and follow through by exploring how you can respond to poverty and hunger in terms of political policy, perhaps through advocacy groups such as "Bread for the World."

CHAPTER FIVE
LIVING BY FORGIVENESS

"Forgive us our debts as we forgive our debtors."

It has been said that one of the most observable doctrinal realities is the reality of sin. Even though process theology affirms the "original wholeness" of creation and God's redemptive and transformative presence in every moment of life, I'm fully convinced that sin and pain vie with beauty and love as realities we experience on a daily basis. However, we define it, we live in a world of beauty, reflective of divine creative wisdom, which is tragically marred by alienation, brokenness, hate, passivity, bullying, and aggression. On a daily basis, national leaders threaten war; children are shot at elementary schools; toddlers are separated from the refugee parents; and hunters purposely murder endangered species. God seeks wholeness and adventure in every moment of our lives, and yet often we miss the mark, preferring stability to creative transformation and self-interest to world loyalty. If we look in the mirror of our lives, there are times when we must confess in the words of the cartoon strip Pogo, written during the Vietnam War – we have met the enemy and it is us!

With each "breaking news" report, we realize that death, pain, and injustice — much of it human-caused — detracts from God's dream for the world. We struggle with regrets, grudges, and words we'd like to take back, as well as courage we wish we had embodied in difficult situations. We also see the brokenness of the USA in its polarization, incivility, normalization of racism and hate speech, and neglect of strangers, the vulnerable and the environment. The pervasiveness of sin as a social reality, a relational ill passed on from generation to generation, affects us all. Process theology responds to the reality of sin with a prophetic voice grounded in God's vision of Shalom and challenging social and political systems that perpetrate injustice, violence, and ecological destruction.

Sin is real and so are the grudges we feel and the burdens we bear. We need forgiveness, and we need to forgive. We need a grace greater than ourselves to live by forgiveness in a world of pain. We need to be able to trust a Loving Reality that brings forth tragic beauty from the suffering and alienation that characterize our lives and social relationships.

Each Sunday, at the congregation where I serve as pastor, we pray "forgive us our trespasses as we forgive those who trespass against us." We all know something about trespassing because most of us have seen and disobeyed "no trespassing" signs — especially on the beach! We show up where we don't belong. We break rules. We violate boundaries often set up for our own well-being and have trouble getting back home again.

As a Baptist, I grew up a "debtor." In our Baptist theology, we owe God for our misdeeds. We have violated God's law, we have disrespected our Creator, and we need to pay the bill. We have maxed out our moral credit cards and have no goodness of our own to redeem our debt. In the course of our lives, other people have hurt us and justice must be done. An eye for an eye and a tooth for a tooth and getting revenge or seeing the suffering of those who hurt us often feels good. On May 2, 2011, after walking the grounds of Bethany College in West Virginia, where I was giving a series of lectures, I returned to my room, turned on NPR and the 6:30 a.m. news reported, "Osama bin Laden has been killed." I let out a "Hallelujah" and made a fist pump - I was glad no one was awake to see it! Justice done, the world made right. But, really? Yes, Osama's dead, but that won't restore the 3000 who died as result of attacks on 9/11. Two decades of war in Afghanistan can never fully compensate for the grief of friends and families and our ongoing fear of terrorism. Our war of retribution has led to further violence with no end in sight.

There are times that we can't repair the damage, and we need to hear from God, "You are forgiven." Or someone we love needs to say to us, "That hurt me, but I choose to love you any way."

Other liturgies invoke the word "sin" to describe the obvious waywardness of the human condition. Sin, as missing the mark, not fulfilling our potential, harming ourselves or another. Sin is revealed in our turning away from God in disobedience or by harming one of God's creatures. We can begin again, and we

24

often do, but we can't undo the past. It is "a true fact," even if it leads to greater insight and healing. We need repentance, repair, and renewal. We need to take another path back to God's vision for us and the world.

In praying for forgiveness, we confess that we can't hide from God. As Psalm 139 proclaims, God searches us and knows us fully. Yet, in being known by God, we can admit our mistakes, say we're sorry and mean it and begin again. Like the loving father and mother, God is willing to welcome every prodigal child. But, more than that, God runs out to meet us, broken as we are, and like the good shepherd, God searches all night long to bring us safely home.

Sin is ultimately about our relationship with God and others. When we sin, we hurt others – the earth and its creatures and our fellow humans – and we also hurt God, the Open Heart of the Universe. God truly feels the pain we inflict on others. Our sins against creatures ultimately bring pain to our Creator. The One who brings forth galaxies and species is also, as Whitehead says, "the fellow sufferer who understands."

Still, despite the reality of sin, we live in an environment of grace in which God is constantly calling us from alienation to reconciliation. We have received grace, and the only choice we have is to forgive others as difficult as it is. How many times shall we forgive, Jesus was asked? Seven times seven, he responded – and in the numerology of that time – forever without limit. Forgiveness doesn't mean forgetting or being a spiritual or emotional doormat. Grace and forgiveness give us the courage to face injustice squarely and say "this is wrong. Stop!"

Forgiveness is tough and sometimes we can't forgive– the pain is too great. I can assure you if another has traumatized, abused, debased, or maligned you, there may be hurts that you personally can't forgive. Forgiveness doesn't mean you let criminals grow free or let leaders do as they wish. Forgiveness is preventative as well as responsive. So, we say "no" to a bully and help a friend leave an abusive relationship; we challenge unjust systems or poverty that lead to homelessness; we pray and also picket. Following Jesus means preventing sin and pain, not just soothing it. It may also lead to restorative justice that focuses on the healing of persons who have been hurt in personal relationships or by unjust social systems.

We must forgive – to let the burden go - to be healthy again, to move forward, to be part of the healing of another. Unforgiveness creates a barrier between God and ourselves, limiting possibilities and miring us in the past. When we close our hearts to others, we close ourselves to God's dream for our lives and prevent God from becoming fully present as our companion and guide. Unforgiveness shrinks our world to the alienation we experience. Jesus' parable of the unforgiving servant, reminds us that we all have fallen short and when we fail to forgive others, we heap further burdens of pain upon ourselves. Forgiveness opens us to a wide array of divine possibilities and enables God to do new and creative things in our lives. What we do truly shapes God's ability to transform our live, enhancing or minimizing God's ability to shape our experience.

But, what about the sins of nations? In Jesus' parable of the sheep and the goats, the nations of the world must face divine judgment. There is only realm and though Reinhold Niebuhr rightly points out the tension between "moral man and immortal society," nations are also measured by God's quest for Shalom. The biblical tradition challenges national leaders and business tycoons to confess the sins of greed, injustice, and violence. Yet, such national confession is deemed a sign of weakness and a threat to national sovereignty. Still, as a nation, we have much to confess and our failure both to confess our national sins – slavery and racism, the genocide of First Americans, annexing of Mexican territory, and tax practices that widen the gap between the rich and poor, separation of children from their refugee parents – threatens the soul of the nation.

Our greatest moments involved our willingness to confront our nation's original sin of slavery; forgive and rebuild nations that had been our military adversaries, in particular Japan and Germany; and presidential speeches, such as that of George W. Bush, who clearly distinguished between Muslim terrorists and peaceful practitioners of Islam following the attacks on 9/11. Process theology affirms that moments of national "truth and reconciliation" awaken a nation to greater possibilities for justice and well-being. Whether personal or corporate, confession and forgiveness, repentance and reparation, evoke the healing power of God that creatively transforms relationships, communities, and the planet.

LIVING THE PRAYER OF JESUS

We always have the opportunity to "live by forgiveness." Yet, such liberating forgiveness requires self-awareness and the willingness to change our attitudes and behaviors. In this exercise, begin with a few minutes of silent prayer, breathing in God's ambient providence. Trusting God's providence, make a moral inventory – what is often called an Examen – in which you reflect on persons from whom you are alienated. Explore the pain you feel and the impact on your life. After a few minutes, reflect on persons you may have hurt and who may have grievances against you. Visualize God's light shining in and through those from whom you are alienated and those who may bear grudges against you. Ask God to guide you toward way that might promote reconciliation.

In a similar fashion, reflect prayerfully on the sins of our nation. Where do we fall short of God's vision of Shalom? What is the impact of our nation sins? Confess the sins of our nation and ask for God's guidance in terms of ways that you as a citizen can bring healing and justice to our national life.

CHAPTER SIX
FROM TEMPTATION
TO TRANSFORMATION

"Lead us not into temptation but deliver us from evil."

This is the question that inspired me to deliver the sermon series that led to the writing of this book. One of our long-term members shared her confusion about a loving God leading people into temptation. "How can a loving God tempt us to do bad things?" she asked. "Do we need protection from God?"

To many of us the notion of God tempting us seems inconceivable. If God is loving and good, why would God be the source temptations that might lead to our personal or professional undoing? Why would God bring us to trial, and test us, knowing that we fail more often than succeed – or just barely get by, often hurting ourselves and others – in difficult times?

This is a legitimate question to ask, especially from the perspective of process theology for whom God's unambiguous quest for healing and beauty is central. Process theology does not assume that God predestines every event, or that God divides the world in the saved and damned. In a world of multiple – indeed, myriad – actors, God seeks, as Alfred North Whitehead asserts, the best for each particular moment of experience, given the impact of our previous actions and the environment around of us. At times the best for this moment – this impasse – may appear "bad" compared to the ideals toward which we aspire.

We must deal with temptation, regardless of its source, as a ubiquitous reality, not unlike the reality of sin. In the wake of temptation are broken marriages, dishonest business dealings, health crises, addictions, and automobile accidents, not to mention the seductions of power that lead to government sanctioned violence and trauma.

"Lead us not into temptation" sounds like divine "entrapment," putting us in situations where we are likely to make harmful mistakes. If God is intentionally the source of temptation, how can we trust God's love for us? If God is helping us one day, and hurting us another, how can we know when God is on our side or if what we are experiencing, when we turn our back on what's best for us and others, is God's will or our own desires? Instead of passing the buck as comedian Flip Wilson did with his excuse, "the devil made me do it," we can excuse our mistakes with "God made me do it." God provided the negative lure and I just went with it. Or, as Exodus suggests, God "hardened" Pharaoh's heart, thus inspiring choices that led to the divine slaughter of the Egyptian first born along with the liberation of the Hebrew people.

All of us know what it's like to be tempted. Who hasn't been tempted to choose the lesser path or a behavior we know is harmful to body, soul, or relationships. Who hasn't turned their back on what Abraham Lincoln describes as "the better angels of our nature." The apostle Paul confesses, "For I do not do the good I want, but the evil I do not want is what I do." (Romans 17:19) Or as the old adage goes, everything good in life is immoral, illegal, or fattening.

As a process theologian, I believe that God is on our side. Accordingly, in my pastoral ministry, I avoid using maxims such as "God never gives you a problem you can't handle" or "God is testing me with cancer or failure." I don't believe God causes cancer or guides us to make wrong decisions. I don't believe God is out to get us; I believe God is out to love us.

Now some versions of the Lord's prayer have tried to reinterpret the suggestion that God causes temptation. The New Zealand prayer book paraphrases:

> In times of temptation and test, spare us.
> From the grip of all that is evil, free us.

Philip Newell's "Casa del Sol" prayer implores:

> Don't forsake us in times of conflict but lead us to new beginnings...

While these versions appropriately soften God's involvement in temptation, there still is an element of threat embedded in them. Testing and temptation are pervasive and we can fail despite our best efforts to walk the right path. We can be corrupted despite our attempts to be moral.

Temptation is real and becomes more challenging as we move from childhood to adulthood. Scripture suggests that God's Spirit sent Jesus to the desert to test his vocation and commitment to God's realm. In the desert, Jesus was tempted by good things — food, power, and security. Yet, even good things can be abused when they get in the way of better things. Food is intended to be enjoyed. Yet, we can overeat and eat the wrong foods. We can put our health at risk and have diets whose production leads to hunger and poverty among other people. Power is good but power can be destructive. Politicians bully and bloviate and can subvert constitutional law trying to achieve their policy goals or maintain control. Security is good but if it is our highest good, every stranger is a threat and diversity is dangerous.

Life is ambiguous: our greatest strengths can be source of our undoing. Moreover, every achievement has a challenge hidden within. We rejoice in technology, but what was intended to be labor saving makes for 24/7 lives in which we never get down time. We are delighted at the use of internet and social media but it can be employed to undermine our political system, and for bullying and cyberwarfare. We like having the news at our disposal: but "breaking news" every fifteen minutes heightens our anxiety and weakens our ability to discern the difference between fact and falsehood.

Process theology is clear that God does not directly cause suffering or evil, whether personal or natural. Still in the temptations we experience, God is implicated. Whitehead notes that the best for a particular "impasse" may not be ideal, but may involve pain and struggle, especially if we consistently turned away from God's vision.

Process theologian Bernard Loomer once stated that ambiguity should be a primary theological theme. At times, even God's vision of Shalom and human creativity may be ambiguous. Cosmic adventure involves destruction as well as creation. God's creativity opens the door to human freedoms that can hurt as well as heal and harm as well as help. Had evolution stopped at single cell organisms, no one would worry about global climate change. Had God radically limited human ingenuity, we wouldn't be talking about nuclear war or genetically modified foods that may modify us!

Temptation and spiritual growth. "Lead us not into temptation but deliver us from evil." Perhaps, we need to go back to the fatherhood and motherhood of God to better understand God's role in the challenges and temptations we experience. I know what it's like to be a parent and grandparent, and being good parent often means putting limits on children and youth that seem painful at first. Good parenting also involves creating — or allowing — certain challenges to help them grow. How many of us had to overcome our children's tears to help them learn to ride a bike or swim? How many of us had to withdraw our help so that they could do a task on their own? Parenting may not mean making life easy for your children, and your decisions may seem harsh to your children, even if no direct ill is intended. But, every positive parent knows that growth requires push and pull. A good parent, however, ensures as much as possible that their child succeeds by her or his own efforts by not creating impossible situations, by respecting her or his level of maturity, and by constructing a playground to encourage maximal freedom and creativity with as little risk as possible.

God is the best of parents, and like a good parent, God cannot overcome our freedom and must – along with us – deal with the consequences of our actions. We may choose against God's vision. We may decide not to grow, or we may use our new achievements for self-interest, but every step of the way God is seeking to overcome — to deliver us — from the evils we might knowingly or unknowingly create.

God's way is that of Shalom, justice, joy, and peace: the evolutionary and moral arc is aimed at Shalom for us and the world. Yet, divine challenges may seem painful: it is challenging when your values are questioned, it is painful to struggle and succeed one day at a time with addiction, your personal and moral muscles ache when you try be a better person, it is depressing to discover that your nation is on the wrong side of domestic and foreign policy issues such that you can no longer pray for national success. In such moments, God is not just the source of calm but the engine of novelty and progress, and healing and wholeness. Amid the challenges and struggles, God is with us, giving us chances time after time, so that we might in all the ambiguity of life, seek God's realm on earth as it is in heaven and find our wholeness in a realm where tragedy is transformed by beauty, and love wins the day.

LIVING THE PRAYER OF JESUS

The Jesuit tradition employs the Examen, or examination of conscience, as a means of self-awareness. At the end of the day – or throughout the day – you stop to ask in a meditative fashion, "Where is God in my life? Are my decisions moving me closer or further away from God's vision for my life?" Conclude by asking for God's forgiveness and guidance for the day ahead.

In my version of the Examen, I invite you to explore the following pattern, taking from five to ten minutes depending on your timeframe:

Quiet prayer, breathing in God's peace, presence, and possibility.

Thanksgiving for God's blessings.

Ask God to "search" and "reveal" where we are this day.

Reflect on your experiences, feelings, and actions, in light of God's vision for your life.

Ask for grace and forgiveness.

Reflect on your nation's actions and values.

Ask for grace, forgiveness, and guidance in terms of ways you can support your nation's "better angels."

Conclude with a prayer of thanksgiving and guidance for the day ahead.

32

CHAPTER SEVEN
THE POWER TO HEAL

"For thine is the kingdom and the power and the glory
forever and ever. Amen."

In some ways, life really is all about power, whether we're talking about politics, relationships, or religious life. A presidential candidate refers to his opponents as "losers" and, once elected, bullies anyone who opposes his policies. Leaders assert "might is right," without regard to morality or the long-term consequences of their actions. A legendary football coach proclaims, "winning isn't everything, it's the only thing." And, of course, we have been counseled by Lord Acton that "power tends to corrupt and absolute power corrupts absolutely." Can there be such a thing as holy and loving power, whether divine, corporate, or personal?

Life is about power, and power is about the ability to affect changes in our world, to get things done, to achieve your goals, to exert an influence on other people. But, as Lord Acton notes, power is seductive and most of us want our own way even if the power and well-being of others, on small or large scale, must be sacrificed. It takes a good deal of maturity to love others as yourself, to wish others success when they are competitors, and to move from individualism and nation-first to world loyalty and sacrificial love.

I believe that the Lord's Prayer presents us with a different version of power than we usually see in business, politics, personal relationships, and the affairs of nations. It is the power of community, humility, perseverance, courage, and love.

One of my theological mentors, process theologian Bernard Loomer, spoke of two kinds of power – unilateral and relational - and in many ways, this binary understanding of power describes the power dynamics of our world. The most common understanding of power is unilateral power. This is one-sided power grounded in control, coercion, and independence. We all know this kind

33

of power — it is the power of the boss who says "my way or the highway." The leader who demands absolute obedience, or "heads will roll." The parent who refuses to listen to his child and yells, "because I said so." This is the power of "win-lose" relationships, of domination, of silencing opposition. Unilateral power is easily misused: we see it in the rise of the "me, too" movement challenging the power of men to assault and diminish women employees and companions; we see it in a government that intentionally separates refugee children from parents, regardless of the long term trauma; we see it in leaders who threaten nuclear war or the annihilation of those who criticize them.

Unilateral power is "one-way" power it acts but does not receive. It prizes radical individualism. It shapes but does not allow itself to be moved by the joy or pain or others. It is the power of a god who creates and determines but never truly experiences or responds to the creaturely world.

Unilateral power is often touted as strength, and leaders often perpetuate policies and don't back down because they don't want to be perceived as weak. But, unilateral and coercive power is ultimately weak and brittle. It acts, but doesn't have the courage to listen to other viewpoints. It appears to win, because it's afraid to share. It is afraid to change course even when better options are available.

There is, Loomer asserted, another kind of power, the power of relationships, grounded in listening, opening to new ideas, affirming others' creativity, and embracing others' experiences. This is the power of looking at the long haul and not short-term gain. It is the power of win-win partnerships in which your gain is mine as well. Such power is evident in Paul's description of Christ in Philippians:

> Let the same mind be in you that was in Christ Jesus,
> who, though he was in the form of God,
> did not regard equality with God as something
> to be exploited, but emptied himself, taking
> the form of a slave, being born in human likeness.
> And being found in human form,

he humbled himself and became obedient
to the point of death—even death on a cross.

Therefore God also highly exalted and gave him the
name that is above every name,so that at the name
of Jesus every knee should bend, in heaven
and on earth and under the earth, and every
tongue should confess that Jesus Christ is Lord,
to the glory of God the Father. (Philippians 2:5-11)

According to Paul, Christ could have vanquished his foes, he could have lorded it over the world and separated the world into winners and losers and saved and unsaved, but his power is manifest sacrificial love that wins the day through healing, empathy, and community.

Paul's listeners would have been amazed at the contrast between Christ's power and Caesar's – "every knee bows to Caesar" out of fear – failure to bend the knee means persecution and death; every knee bows to Jesus out of love, there is no failure for each one is cherished despite her or his sin, and the power of Jesus' apparent weakness outlasts Caesar, Napoleon, Mussolini, Stalin, Hitler, and the would-be tyrants of our time.

Our vision of divine power shapes our image of human power. Have the mind of Christ,

Paul counsels. Imagine a world in which everyone has a voice, everyone matters, in which winning involves helping everyone realize their identity as God's beloved child exploring their gifts in a supportive community.

Luther was wrong in separating the sacred and secular realms of life. While nations and municipalities may have to use forms of coercion to keep the peace and protect national sovereignty, there is only one kingdom and that is the kingdom of love. Glory is not found in the victory of the few or the defeat of the foe but the eventual victory of all God's children. The glory of God, so said the church father Irenaeus, is a human being, fully alive. God's glory is manifest the power to create a beautiful, evolving, spectacular universe, that brings forth galaxies and planets, stars and starfish, right whales and little babies. God has the whole world in his hands and

God's created a world in which power includes, embraces, inspires, and heals. Governments may need a "big stick" from time to time, but they should also speak softly and seek reconciliation rather than annihilation. Borders need to be protected, but with compassion and care, rather than violence and traumatization.

We seem to be a long way from God's kingdom "on earth as it is in heaven." Our planet seems to be slipping into self-interest and cheap patriotism rather than care for the vulnerable and loyalty to the planet. People use religion as a form of oppression, hard-heartedness and bullying, and as we observe the 24-hour news cycle, our hopes for the future diminish. But even in challenging times, the Lord's Prayer presents a different way of life, the way of Jesus, moving slowly yet persistently toward justice and freedom, the power of God, incarnate in the better angels of our nature. The Lord's Prayer challenges us to experience God's vision in our daily lives and the affairs of nation; to trust God with our futures; and to live – even in business and government – guided by relational rather than coercive power. As Theodore Parker proclaimed: "We cannot understand the moral Universe. The arc is a long one, and our eyes reach but a little way; we cannot calculate the curve and complete the figure by the experience of sight; but we can divine it by conscience, and we surely know that it bends toward justice. Justice will not fail, though wickedness appears strong, and has on its side the armies and thrones of power, the riches and the glory of the world, and though poor men crouch down in despair. Justice will not fail and perish out from the world of men, nor will what is really wrong and contrary to God's real law of justice continually endure."

"Thy kingdom come, thy will be done...for thine is the power and glory forever." This is the kingdom of God, the glory of salvation, and the power of love. In the end, the only power that matters in this fragile and interdependent universe, the power to heal.

LIVING THE PRAYER OF JESUS

We conclude our time with an adventure in holy imagination, or visualization. Begin with a moment of stillness, breathing deeply the energy and wisdom of God. Let God's loving wisdom fill you with every breath. Feel that holy breath connecting you with all creation. Now, visualize God's peaceable kingdom as you perceive it today. What would the world look like if God's realm was embodied on earth as it is in heaven? See the world as you imagine God would want it to be- at the global, national, communal, and interpersonal levels.

Conclude by giving thanks for the gift of vision, and in the spirit of Hillel the Elder's counsel – if not now, when – ask God to show you in the course of your life what first steps you can take to bring heaven to earth in each one of the personal, social, and political realms of life.

QUESTIONS FOR CONVERSATION

I would invite each group to begin with a time of silence, then recite the Lord's Prayer, and read aloud each session's focus passage. I invite you to close each session with prayers

CHAPTER ONE

1. Did you have an opportunity to pray the "New Zealand" version of the Lord's Prayer? What was your response?
2. What is your understanding of prayer? What forms of prayer are most familiar to you? What forms of prayer do you typically practice?
3. Do you agree with the statement "prayer is the ultimate form of connection?" In what ways have you experienced prayer as connecting you with others and with God?
4. What role has the Lord's Prayer played in your own spiritual life?
5. Reflect on the various aspects of prayer cited - "wow!", "thanks!", "help!", "sorry," "inspire," "awaken," and "connect." Which aspects have been most pivotal in your prayer life? Can you think of everyday examples of each prayer focus?
6. In what ways does prayer increase your personal stature? How might prayerfulness take us beyond self-interest to care for others?
7. Where do you personally need prayer today? Where does your congregation need prayer?

CHAPTER TWO

1. Read Philip Newell's Casa del Sol Prayer of Jesus. In what ways does this prayer enhance your experience of the Lord's Prayer?
   "Ground of all being, Mother of life, Father of the universe, Your name is sacred, beyond speaking.

May we know your presence, may your longings
be our longings in heart and in action.
may there be food for the human family today and for the whole
earth community.
Forgive us the falseness of what we have done as we forgive those
who are untrue to us.
Do not forsake us in our time of conflict
but lead us into new beginnings.
for the light of life, the vitality of life, and the
glory of life are yours now and for ever.
Amen.

2. What words do you use to describe God? What do you think of "Father" as a description of God? What are the limits to paternal images of God?

3. What does it mean to "hallow" God's name?

4. Where do you see persons taking God's name in vain? Is taking God's name in vain merely a matter of swearing or are their some more important ways that we deface the divine name?

5. Do you believe that God feels our joy and pain? Why is it important that God be relational and thus involved in our lives rather than distant from the world? Do you think that what we do really makes a difference to God? If so, what difference do our lives make to the quality of God's life and scope of God's work in the world?

CHAPTER THREE

1. What does abundant life mean to you? What are the characteristics of abundance?

2. What things do you perceive as "sacred?" What things do you perceive as "secular?" How do you perceive the relationship of these realms?

3. When you think of heaven, what images come to mind?

4. How do you distinguish between "heaven" and "earth?" In what ways are they similar or different? If God is everywhere, is there a qualitative difference between heaven and earth?

5. How do you understand the "will" of God? Do we have a role in bringing about the will of God?
6. What would it mean to bring the values of heaven to earth?

CHAPTER FOUR

1. What's your favorite kind of bread?
2. Have you ever worried about your "daily bread?" What was the situation you faced? Can you identify with persons for whom issues of hunger are a daily reality?
3. What demeaning terms have you heard about persons who are homeless or poor? Do you think these terms are accurate? Do you think that poverty is often the result of accidental events or bad luck and the decisions of business and governmental agencies? How should we best respond to poverty?
4. Do you ever feel anxious about your financial situation?
5. What are your greatest concerns about the future? Where do you experience peace as you face the future?
6. How might our wealth be connected to the poverty of others? In what ways can we address global as well as local hunger?

CHAPTER FIVE

1. How do you understand sin? Is it inherent in human nature (original) or is it a social reality?
2. What sins do you think are most harmful? Is sin primarily individual or corporate? How do institutions perpetuate sin? Can nations commit sins?
3. In the language of the Lord's Prayer, which do you prefer "debts," "trespasses," or "sins?" Why?
4. Why is forgiveness essential for our spiritual well-being? What are the costs of unforgiveness?
5. Is it possible to heal the past? In what ways is forgiveness transformative of the past?
6. How do we respond to sins that we can't forgive? Can we experience healing even when we can't forgive another for our traumas?

7. In what ways can we "restore" people who have experienced injustice?

CHAPTER SIX

1. How do you understand the statement "lead us not into temptation?" Does God have a role in creating temptations?
2. Where do you see temptation enacted in our culture today? What things are most tempting to you and those around you?
3. Whitehead says that God seeks the best for each moment of experience, and that the best may not always be good. Do you think the quest for perfection often keeps us for achieving good results? Do you think the "best" may not be very good at times? What are situations in which the "best" may not be very good?
4. How do you understand the notion that we are typically tempted by "good" things?
5. The author suggests that God is implicated in some of the evils we experience; suffering is partly the result of God's evolutionary quest for more complex creatures with greater freedom for good and evil. What do you think of this suggestion?

CHAPTER SEVEN

1. How do you understand the nature of divine power? Is God's power primarily relational or unilateral?
2. Where have you seen the misuse of power? Where have you seen power used for good?
3. How do you understand "glory?" What does the glory of God mean to you?
4. How do you understand the nature of power in Philippians 2:5-11?
5. How do our understandings of divine power shape our understandings of human power?
6. Where do you see the "moral arc" of the universe heading? How do you respond to situations that seem to deflect God's

moral arc in history? In what ways might God adapt to our interference with God's vision of Shalom?

TEXTS ON THE LORD'S PRAYER

John Dominic Crossan, *The Greatest Prayer: Rediscovering the Revolutionary Message of the Lord's Prayer.* San Francisco: Harper One, 2010.

Robert Cornwall, *Ultimate Allegiance: The Subversive Nature of the Lord's Prayer.* Gonzales, FL: Energion Publications, 2010.

N.T. Wright, *The Lord and His Prayer.* Grand Rapids, MI: Wm. Eerdmans, 1996.

John Shelby Spong, *Honest Prayer.* Morristown, NJ: Christianity for the Third Millennium, 1993.

TOPICAL LINE DRIVES
Straight to the Point in under 44 Pages

All Topical Line Drives volumes are priced at $5.99 print and $2.99 in all ebook formats.

Available

(The titles of planned volumes may change before release.)

Generous Quantity Discounts Available
Dealer Inquiries Welcome
Energion Publications — P.O. Box 841
Gonzalez, FL 32560
Website: http://energionpubs.com
Phone: (850) 525-3916

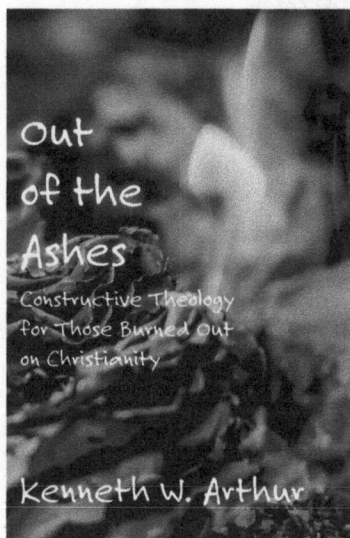

The book is theologically rich, ministerially practical, and is a unique contribution to the continuing discussion regarding progressive Christianity.

C. Drew Smith
Author of *Reframing a Relevant Faith*

ALSO BY BRUCE EPPERLY

I asked Bruce Epperly for an introduction to process theology in 12,000 words. I didn't think he could do it.

He did.

Henry Neufeld, Publisher

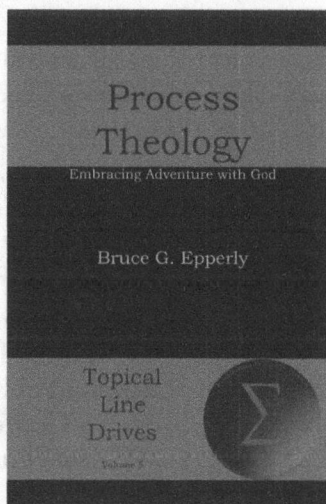

MORE FROM ENERGION PUBLICATIONS

Personal Study

Holy Smoke! Unholy Fire	Bob McKibben	$14.99
The Jesus Paradigm	David Alan Black	$17.99
When People Speak for God	Henry Neufeld	$17.99
The Sacred Journey	Chris Surber	$11.99

Christian Living

Faith in the Public Square	Robert D. Cornwall	$16.99
Grief: Finding the Candle of Light	Jody Neufeld	$8.99
Crossing the Street	Robert LaRochelle	$16.99
Life in the Spirit	J. Hamilton Weston	$12.99

Bible Study

Learning and Living Scripture	Lentz/Neufeld	$12.99
Inspiration: Hard Questions, Honest Answers	Alden Thompson	$29.99
Colossians & Philemon	Allan R. Bevere	$12.99
Ephesians: A Participatory Study Guide	Robert D. Cornwall	$9.99

Theology

Christian Archy	David Alan Black	$9.99
The Politics of Witness	Allan R. Bevere	$9.99
Ultimate Allegiance	Robert D. Cornwall	$9.99
From Here to Eternity	Bruce Epperly	$5.99
The Journey to the Undiscovered Country	William Powell Tuck	$9.99
Eschatology: A Participatory Study Guide	Edward W. H. Vick	$9.99
The Adventist's Dilemma	Edward W. H. Vick	$14.99

Ministry

Clergy Table Talk	Kent Ira Groff	$9.99
Thrive	Ruth Fletcher	$14.99
Out of the Office: A Theology of Ministry	Bob Cornwall	$9.99

Generous Quantity Discounts Available
Dealer Inquiries Welcome
Energion Publications — P.O. Box 841
Gonzalez, FL_ 32560
Website: http://energionpubs.com
Phone: (850) 525-3916

www.ingramcontent.com/pod-product-compliance
Lightning Source LLC
Chambersburg PA
CBHW011746020426
42331CB00014B/3296